The Cat Book

THE
CAT BOOK

by Marianne Besser

Illustrated by Shannon Stirnweis

XEROX EDUCATION PUBLICATIONS
Middletown, Connecticut

for KRISTA

because she loves cats and I love her

Contents

The Cat Book

Most People Like Cats—
Some Don't

MORE PEOPLE SEEM TO ARGUE over cats than over any other animal in the world. People either love or hate cats; they seldom feel indifferent about them.

Throughout history the cat has been either worshiped or feared, pampered or persecuted. Today cats are our most popular pets; there may be as many as fifty million that have homes. Although many people like cats, there are still quite a few who are cat-haters, or are afraid of cats.

Cats have caused trouble even in the same family. The great English writer Thomas Carlyle adored cats, but his wife couldn't stand them. (She liked dogs.) Carlyle kept a black cat and Mrs. Carlyle kept a white dog. The couple often argued about their pets—but the cat and dog got along wonderfully.

Writers, artists, and children usually like cats. They praise their beauty, grace, and cuddlyness. Mark Twain, the author of

Huckleberry Finn, had a great fondness for cats. He once said, "A home without a cat may be a perfect home perhaps, but how can it prove its title?" Other famous Americans who loved cats were Benjamin Franklin, Abraham Lincoln, and President Theodore Roosevelt. Slippers, President Theodore Roosevelt's cat, would vanish for days and weeks at a time, but he always managed to turn up just before big diplomatic dinners. Nobody knows how he knew about the dinners, but he never missed one.

Dr. Albert Schweitzer, the doctor who gave his life to healing the sick and poor in Africa, loved cats. Once when his cat Sizi slept cuddled against his right arm, he wrote with his left hand to avoid waking her. Mohammed, the great prophet who started

the Moslem religion, did something more surprising for his beloved cat Muezza. There is a story that one day Muezza fell asleep on the sleeve of Mohammed's robe. The prophet was suddenly called to a meeting. He so cherished his cat that he cut off the sleeve of his robe so as not to disturb her.

In Thailand, the country Siamese cats come from, most of the people are Buddhists, who revere white animals. If they see a white Siamese cat in the street, they bow to it.

But some people feel quite different about the cat. Napoleon, Brahms, and Shakespeare were among famous persons who disliked cats. Napoleon was so afraid of them that the mere mention of a cat made him tremble.

There are many reasons why people don't like cats. Some think they bring bad luck. Others say that cats' faces are creepy or that their eyes look scary in the dark. There are all kinds of superstitions about cats. Black cats are thought to bring either good luck or bad luck. Some people believe that a black cat crossing your path means bad luck, but that you can turn this into good luck if you jump over it.

In some parts of England people still believe that a cat's tail can cure sore eyes. In Russia they often put a cat in a cradle before a newborn baby is placed in it; this is supposed to drive away all evil spirits. Another superstition says that if a bride-to-be hears a cat sneeze the night before her wedding, she is bound to have a happy marriage. In Kansas there is a superstition that a cat of tortoiseshell color protects its owner against fire. In New England a white cat is supposed to bring poverty to its master. Some Japanese sailors like to keep a three-colored tomcat to ward off evil spirits.

Cats are also supposed to be able to foretell the weather, and, as we shall see later, they are at least sensitive to oncoming storms. Some people believe that a cat washing its face before breakfast forecasts rain; others say exactly the opposite, that it means fine weather. In Maine they even think they can tell what direction the wind will blow according to the way a cat holds its tail.

We know that all of this isn't so. But is there perhaps something about the nature of the cat that creates so many different opinions about this little animal? Does it come from a feeling people have that they have never really tamed the cat?

Wild Cats and Tame

MILLIONS OF YEARS AGO THE small cat we now call the house cat roamed the earth just like its big, wild cousins, the lions and tigers. Even today the house cat has some wild traits, like stalking and hunting other animals.

All the many different kinds of cats in the world belong to the family of Felidae, the felines. They have the same animal ancestor. Before people lived on the earth but after the dinosaurs became extinct, there were still no felines as we know them; no tigers, lions, or house cats. At that time, 40 million years ago, there was an animal called Miacis. Miacis had a long body and short legs. He may have looked a bit like a weasel. Scientists believe that from Miacis came the civets and that the cat family evolved from these.

There are now about fifty different kinds of felines. The lion is the biggest cat. The smallest is the spotted cat of India. It grows only 16 inches long, while the average length of the house cat, without counting its tail, is 19 inches. There are no cats in the

BOBCAT

polar regions, but some kind of cat lives in all the other parts of the world. The lion likes to hunt in the plains of Africa, the tiger stalks the jungles of Asia and Africa. In North and South America we have jaguars, pumas, and smaller wildcats like the lynx.

These are the names of only a few of the different wildcats. The house cat, which now shares its home with people all over the world, has some of the wild traits of one or the other of its feline cousins.

16

Wild Cats and Tame

In the hunt this gentle pet looks as fierce as any jungle animal. Imagine looking at a striped cat through a magnifying glass! Watch it stalk softly through the grass on its padded paws. See it crouch, then jump. It would look much like a tiger stalking through the jungle foliage, pursuing its prey. Later, when it has caught its mouse, the house cat plays with it, just as the spotted leopard plays with his prey.

Like the leopard, the house cat likes to climb trees; it enjoys finding a branch on which it can curl up and go to sleep. A leopard will even pounce on his prey right from the branch of a tree. Indeed, all cats are tree climbers except the very big lion and tiger, which are too heavy for this fun.

Tigers, cats, and jaguars will hiss and spit at enemies or when they are afraid. Like the ocelot and cheetah, the cat purrs when it is contented. Some house cats love water and swim regularly; many jaguars and tigers also are keen swimmers.

TIGERS CAN SWIM

All the felines move in much the same way, silently. The buffalo grazing in the jungle grass never hears the killer tiger until it has pounced on his back. A house cat moves just as quietly; before you know it, it leaps on your lap. The mouse taking a quick run out of its hole doesn't hear it either.

Felines walk so quietly because they all have padded paws, with five toes on the front paw and only four on the hind one. They all walk on the tips of their paws only. The claws are the most hooked and the sharpest of all mammal claws.

Lions, tigers, pumas, house cats, and all other felines except the cheetah move alike in other ways. When they want to go fast they trot; for greater speed they bound over long distances. Usually they move their legs in diagonal pairs—that is, if the left hind one moves forward, the right front one moves forward with it. Each hind foot steps precisely into the print of the front foot. If you watch a cat making footprints as it walks in the sand or snow, you will therefore find that when it moves all four legs it leaves fewer footprints than you would expect.

Wild Cats and Tame

The cheetah is the most different of all the felines. It doesn't move like the other cats; it runs, rather like a fast hound dog. A cheetah can run 70 miles an hour. Cheetahs don't have to creep up to their prey and then pounce, like other cats. They can outrun any animal they want to catch, even the fleet-footed antelope. But still the cheetah is a feline and looks a lot like a large domestic cat.

CHEETAH

All the cats really look much alike. They differ in size, in the shapes of their heads, in the arrangement or markings of their fur. Although the bones of the various kinds of cats may be set differently from each others', all the felines' bones are very strong and almost as hard as ivory. This substance, which comes from the tusk of the elephant, is very hard. In all the felines the muscles are very flexible and the skin hangs loosely, which allows them to stretch as they do. From their pointed teeth we can tell that cats are carnivorous, that they eat meat.

It might be fun to make your next trip to the zoo a cat-study trip. Look at the sleek black panther, the patterns of the tiger's stripes and the leopard's spots, the majesty of the lion's mane. This mane, by the way, grows only in captivity. In the jungle, hunting through thickets and brambles keeps the lion's mane closely "clipped." Look too at American wildcats, like the lynx and the bobcat, and notice their short bodies and tall legs and the long tufts of hair on their ears. And yet you will see in all their faces unmistakably that little house cat.

But with all its similarity to the wildcats, the domestic cat doesn't easily become feral, or wild, even when it is abandoned. The house cat likes people and wants to live with them. There have been many stories of cats that lived alone in the woods for as long as two years and still approached people as soon as they came near. A group of campers once left a cat behind them in a lonely campsite. It had disappeared and they just had forgotten about it. A year later a boat landed in the same spot, and the people were immediately greeted by the glad "meow" of the cat.

LION

Tennessee got her name because a young man and his wife found her abandoned in the mountains of that state. They had stopped their car to take a picture of a stream when they heard a plaintive "meow" nearby. Under a bush sat a female kitten about four months old, with sad green eyes. She was so thin that all her ribs were visible through her fur. She hadn't done very well in protecting herself and finding food.

She was afraid of the young couple, but she also wanted to come near them, and she let them pick her up and put her into the car. Once they had her home she did a lot of hissing and spitting and hiding before she got used to them. But today she is the softest, gentlest pet you could want.

Cats and human beings have been together a long time. But how the first cat came to live with men is still a bit of a mystery.

Gods, Devils, and
Household Pets

THE CAT, SAYS A FAMOUS LEG-
end, was created by Noah, the builder of the ark. It seems that
the rats and mice in the ark bred so fast that they threatened to
eat up all the food. So Noah created the cat to get rid of the rats.
In the story he passed his hand over the head of the lioness, and
she sneezed forth a cat.

We know, of course, that this is a fable, and that the cat, like
all living creatures, developed over millions of years. But how
did the cat become tame? Nobody really knows. Most likely the
cat came to men of its own accord. Perhaps a campfire drew the
cat close to a human group; all cats love a cozy fire. Or maybe
cats found out that wherever men settled there were plenty of
rats and mice.

But it's possible that a child first befriended a cat. Perhaps a
boy or girl heard the plaintive mewing of a lost kitten and

brought it home. The kitten was fed and petted and it stayed. Maybe some of its friends also came. A mother cat can have a great many kittens during her lifetime—as many as a hundred or more. So it would not have taken long before a lot of tame cats lived in people's homes. Something like that may have happened in many parts of the world at the same time.

We are really guessing here. We do know, however, that cats were kept as pets in ancient Egypt as long as five thousand years ago. Early pictures made on the tomb of an Egyptian king of that time showed people holding cats on leashes. They may have been used then to hunt marsh birds for Egyptian kings.

Later, about three thousand years ago, the cat's main job in Egypt was to guard the granaries. Egypt was then the grain

capital of the world. Ships came to its ports to take on grain and carry it to countries whose people did not have enough. The cat was very useful to the Egyptians because it kept rats and mice away from the stored food. This meant that the grain could be stored for a long time.

The Egyptian people were grateful to the cat for helping them to become a rich kingdom. They considered the cat sacred, and none were allowed to be taken out of the country. A man lost his head for killing a cat, even accidentally. When a cat died, its owners shaved off their eyebrows in mourning. If there was a fire, an Egyptian saved his cat before his house and furnishings.

The ancient Egyptians had a great civilization. They built beautiful cities with fine temples, palaces, and parks. The tombs for their kings, the pyramids, still stand after thousands of years. Cats had a place everywhere—in temples and palaces, and in poor men's homes too. All cats were well fed and well cared for. But the most pampered ones were the temple cats that protected the Holy Granaries. These cats were thought to be holy and were adorned with jewels. They were fed with bread soaked in milk, and with fish raised in special fish tanks. The Egyptians knew that it wasn't necessary to starve a cat to make her a good mouser. If a cat likes to hunt she will do it on a full stomach as well as an empty one—in fact, better.

When temple cats died, they were embalmed and mummified like Egyptian kings. Their bodies were wrapped in linen bands. Then they were placed inside gilded mummy cases. Little mummies of mice were set about their tombs to keep them happy in the afterlife.

The ancient Egyptians worshiped many different gods and goddesses. Many of these gods had the shape of animals. The cat too became an Egyptian goddess. The name of the cat goddess was Bast, or Pasht. Some say that our modern word "puss" may come from Pasht. Pasht was the goddess of the moon and the chase. She was both good and evil, loving and frightening. The annual festival for Pasht was the grandest of the year. On that day Egyptians traveled many miles over the desert or in boats along the Nile to Pasht's splendid temple at Beni-Hassan. People even brought along their cat mummies to bury them near the shrine.

Egyptians stopped worshiping the cat goddess about 400 A.D. Today most Egyptians are Moslems. They do not worship the cat, but they consider it sacred, along with some other animals.

The cat had its grandest days in ancient Egypt, but it also was valued long ago in other parts of the world. In Japan it was a house pet at least 3,000 years ago. It seems that long ago some kittens were born in the palace of the Emperor of Japan. He was so charmed with these playful, pretty creatures that he ordered his ministers to bring them up with as much care as their own children.

Soon there were lots of cats in Japanese homes. But the Japanese made a big mistake. They thought that the mere presence of a cat would keep mice away, so for a long time cats in Japan were kept on leashes. This was great fun for the mice that nibbled cheese right in front of the leashed cats. But finally the Japanese, overrun with rodents, passed a law that cats must be unleashed and allowed to roam freely.

Cats came to Europe much later. Nobody is quite certain just how or when they arrived. They probably came in various ways. Even though Egyptians had a law against taking cats out of the

country, some no doubt were smuggled out by the traders who came to Egypt for grain. They kept them on their boats and later sold them at European ports for high prices. Some cats were brought to Europe by the monks who came from Egypt to preach Christianity on the Continent.

The Egyptian house cat, the Kaffir cat, was a shorthaired cat with long legs and tawny fur. When it was brought to Europe it may have mated with wildcats already living there, and this may be how we got the many-colored cats that are still the most popular pets both in the Old and the New World.

The Scots were one of the first European peoples to keep cats. Scotland actually was named after Scota, the daughter of an Egyptian pharaoh. Scota's great-grandson, Fergus I, conquered Scotland, gave the land its name and probably its first cats.

The Scots admired the cat not only for its usefulness but also for its bravery. To the Scots the cat became the symbol of courage and strength. Even today when a Scotsman says "cat" he could be talking about a soldier.

The people of Wales, now part of Great Britain, once had a law covering the sale of cats. In the year 948 the Welsh prince

Howel the Good fixed the price of a newborn kitten at one penny. After its eyes were open a kitten cost twopence; a full-grown mouser sold for fourpence. That was a lot of money in those days.

Cats have gone to sea for hundreds of years. Until they took cats on board, European captains always sailed close to shore because they could not keep their food free of rats. But once they had cats, about a thousand years ago, European mariners began to sail great distances. So cats came to America with the first European settlers.

The North American Indians did not keep cats. If they had, they might have been able to settle in one place more easily. Many Indian tribes planted crops and tried to store their food over the winter, but always the mice, rats, and other rodents came and ate it. So the Indians had to move on and go back to hunting for their food. With the help of cats they might have been able to save their grain from the rodents and live long enough in one place to build real towns and cities.

But the settlers who came here from Europe brought cats to protect their stored food. And they needed them, because America has more than 100 kinds of rodents. At first cats were scarce and therefore very valuable in the Americas. Cats were bartered and sold at all kinds of prices. One of the first cats sold in South America brought $560.

Today you often can get a cat free. But that doesn't mean that cats are less useful; only that there are many more of them. We need cats today as much as we ever did. Most cats are mainly pets, but quite a few earn their keep.

Cats Earn Their Keep

CATS ARE USEFUL TO US FOR the same reason that they were useful to the ancient Egyptians. Together with owls, hawks, snakes, and weasels, they help to keep down the number of rats and mice in our country. Rats are very fertile. They breed all the time. In only three years one pair of rats and their descendants can have 600,000 offspring. Even with our modern means of storage, rats still spoil millions of dollars worth of food every year. More cats in the right places would cut down this loss.

Store owners know how useful cats are. Most grocers keep a cat in their store. Often you will see a contented cat curled up in a spot of sun in the butcher's window. When the owner leaves the store at night, he makes sure that the cat is locked up inside. Then he doesn't have to worry all evening long whether the mice will get to the food. In return for its work, the store cat is usually well fed with meat, milk, and fish.

Many cats earn their keep this way in warehouses, stores, and factories—in any place that people want to keep clean and free

33

of rodents. Most farmers have one or more cats around the farm to keep mice and rats under control. There are also firehouse cats that learn how to slide down the pole with the firemen and sit on the engine as they drive to the fire.

Cats protect our very lives. Rats still spread the bubonic plague, the so-called Black Death, of the fourteenth century. India still has many outbreaks of the plague. Most epidemics occur in villages where there are few or no cats. Even an American town had an outbreak of bubonic plague not so long ago. Many cats were brought into the town and soon after, the plague was stilled. Though there may have been other reasons why it ended, the cats almost surely had a part in it.

Even now, when most food on ships is stored under refrigeration, cats are traditional passengers on voyages. Most sailors like

cats. They are good company, and make excellent sailors themselves. Cats never get seasick, and they can keep their balance even on a storm-tossed deck.

Cats have accompanied sea explorers on dangerous voyages. Not long ago, explorer William Willis traveled 7,000 miles on a raft with only a parrot and a cat for company.

Many cats learn to do special jobs for their masters. One man, a garage owner, was saved the expense of special equipment by his cat Rube. This lovely, longhaired tomcat slept in the front of the garage. Whenever a car stopped for gas, Rube clawed at a bell rope that rung over his sleeping cushion. This rang a bell in the workshop where the owner was repairing cars, and he then could come out to serve his customer.

Cats have kept people warm and comforted them in all kinds of situations. During England's Wars of the Roses, Sir Henry Wyat was imprisoned in the Tower of London. One day a cat walked into his cell. Wyat made much of it, petting it and holding it. The story goes that after that the grateful cat brought him a pigeon every day which Wyat had dressed and roasted for his supper. Later, Sir Henry was appointed to high posts at the British Court and always took a faithful cat with him.

During World War II a cat in Russia served as a messenger for a Russian company right in the front line. She carried messages for the soldiers to a house across the battle line, walking with tail uplifted right under screaming bullets.

Most cats do not achieve such heroism. But there are many stories of household cats who saved their sleeping masters from burning by waking them with frantic mewing and clawing.

Our household cats also earn their keep. They do help to keep our own homes free of rodents, but since most of us no longer are threatened by rats and mice, this is only incidental. We appreciate cats because they are delightful company. They are affectionate, beautiful, clean, and are easy pets to keep. They add warmth and charm to any home. Let us take a closer look at the cat to see why this is so.

The Physical Cat

ONE NINE-YEAR-OLD BOY ADmired his cat especially because it could walk all over his shelves without knocking down his model airplanes. Certainly the cat is the most agile and graceful of all mammals. Cats can jump great heights and distances and land exactly where they want to. They are extremely alert and respond with all their senses to the world about them. When they are not asleep, their wide-open clear eyes and pointed ears seem to see and hear everything.

Cats are like this because of the way they are built. Their muscles and bones, their keen sense organs, and their good brain all combine to make them alive and quick.

The cat's body is almost as elastic as rubber. Watch a cat crouch and then catapult forward. It can leap like this, ten feet across a room, to land on a bug. Many cats can jump ten times as far as the length of their bodies, which is about 18-21 inches without the tail. Cats can twist and turn in almost any direction. When a cat cleans itself it can curve its back so far forward that it can lick an outstretched back paw. In this position it is almost

doubled up. Licking its back near its tail is hardly more difficult.

Cats can crouch and curl and stretch like that because they have an unusual system of bones and muscles. The bones are strong and flexible. They are set together with levers in such a way that cats can move them in other directions besides forward and backward. Dogs, for example, can move their bones only back and forth.

You probably have seen a cat arch its back like a mountain. It can do this because its spine is especially flexible. At the same

time, the spine is not very strong; that's why a cat never falls on its back if it can help it. If it starts a fall upside down, a cat can flop over in mid-air and land on its feet. It can do that even when it is dropped only ten inches. If you want to try it, do it over a bed or a couch. Hold your pet in your arms upside down —just for a moment, because cats don't like to be upside down —and drop it gently on the bed. You will see it swivel around and land on its paws.

Because they land on their feet so often, people say cats have nine lives. What they mean is that cats can jump and fall where

a man would be hurt. But cats never jump from very high places unless they are in danger. Everybody has heard of cats that can climb up trees but not down them. Sometimes the fire department comes to the rescue. Sometimes the cat's master has to trick it down. One tomcat climbed a tree and refused to come down until his mistress gently poked him off with a pole. He wasn't hurt but he was badly scared and he never climbed a tree again. His sister cat climbed a tree to an even higher branch. She sat there for a while and then figured out a way of climbing down backward. This is the best way for a cat to climb down a tree, because its claws can hook into the bark for support.

Most of the time, when they fall from places that are not too high, cats land on their feet without breaking any bones. Their flexible muscles let them bounce gently onto the ground. But

cats have been killed falling from high places. If a cat lives in a high apartment it is safest to have screens in the windows so it can't fall out.

The fatty padding on the paws also adds to the cat's springiness. Altogether a cat's paws are very useful in several different ways. Normally cats walk on their toes; their claws are pulled in and never touch the ground. But when a cat needs to grasp a tree or catch a mouse or hook a piece of meat, its claws shoot out. They are curved and sharp and they keep growing like our fingernails.

The Physical Cat

We cut our fingernails when they grow too long; cats have to wear off the edges of their claws as they grow longer. That's what they do when they scratch a log; they are not *sharpening* their claws, as people often think. Some people don't have cats because they fear that they will scratch up the furniture. A cat that goes outside will use trees for scratching, and indoor cats can be trained to use special scratching posts or an old piece of rug.

A cat's back paws are mainly for climbing and fighting, but its front paws are used for grasping, holding and touching, much as we use our hands. With its front paw a cat can poke, bat, catch, hold, and even pull. Some cats eat by dipping their front paws into the food and licking it off. A cat can stun a

mouse by batting it strongly with a paw. Yet a poke with a paw
may be used to show affection.

Paws are also used to test strange new things—to get the feel
of something or to make sure it doesn't move. Cats also feel with
their whiskers and their fur. A cat's whiskers are almost as sensitive as our fingertips. They tell the cat whether an object is hard
or soft, rough or smooth, and how far away it is. They even help
to tell whether another cat is a friend or foe. Fanning out its
whiskers in the dark helps a cat feel its way about and avoid

bumping into objects. Whiskers are very important that way, but they do not measure the space a cat wants to pass through. That is a popular but false notion. If that were true then broadly built cats would always have very long whiskers and cats with narrow shoulders would have short ones, but it is just as often the other way around. If the whiskers did tell the cat about the space it wants to pass through, then cats never would be stuck in tunnels and holes, and that has happened to quite a few cats.

The fur of a cat is also very sensitive, partly because it is full of static electricity. You can see how strongly a cat reacts to even the slightest touch. Take a piece of paper and touch the cat just lightly on its fur and you will see its whole body shiver. The cat's electrified fur makes it very sensitive to changes in atmospheric pressure and thus in the weather; often, before a storm, a cat will pace restlessly through the room. It feels the atmospheric pressure much more than we do. This may explain the superstition that cats can forecast any and all weather, which of course they cannot do.

The cat's hearing is probably its keenest sense, and a cat relies heavily on its ears to find its way around. Cats hear high, shrill, and soft sounds that none of us can hear—the distant squeak of a mouse in the field, the slither of a snake in the grass, the tinkle of a faraway bell. A cat can even judge the different heights and distances from which a sound falls. It will know whether a bird is singing on the first branch of a tree or on another only slightly higher.

Cats can tell fine differences between similar sounds. Many cats can single out the special motor sound of their owner's car from any other that may drive up to the house. A great many cats recognize the special clink of their dishes. One cat that loved eggs would arrive in the kitchen from anyplace in the house any time its mistress cracked an egg.

Cats are quite sensitive about people's voices; they like some and dislike others. Some cats truly enjoy music. One cat rolled around the floor and purred whenever she heard a special favorite melody that her master played on the piano.

Cats often find their way home over long distances, mainly by following familiar sounds. A long time ago in the city of Marseilles in France there was an old tomcat that had lived in a museum all his life. Because he was so old he was taken to the country to die in peace. But he wanted to be in his beloved museum. So he set off one morning and, keeping his ears pricked and turning in all directions, he slowly stalked his way home. The trip took him several weeks in which he must have walked with sad and anxious heart, forever listening. Since he had been taken out of the city inside a box in a horse and buggy, he could not rely on anything he had seen. On his trip back he probably kept moving in the direction of the distant hubbub of the big city.

Once he reached Marseilles, however, he still had to find his way to the museum. All the time, as he stalked silently through the streets, he listened for something special, for the chime he had heard every day for over ten years—the museum clock. Marseilles was full of bell sounds and clock chimes, but finally he singled out the chime of the museum clock; and soon he was home, where he remained content for many years.

Though this cat relied mostly on his hearing, once in Marseilles he also must have used his nose to smell his way back home. A cat's sense of smell is not as keen as a dog's, but it is much more delicate. Sometimes a cat will pull down the branch of a tree to smell its blossoms. Cats like sweet smells such as those of flowers and perfumes. Generally they do not like pungent odors such as strong soaps and disinfectants. Let a city cat loose in a country garden and it will go dizzy with the delightful smells; it may run from flower to flower, wiggling its nose and rolling about. A favorite aroma is given out by catnip, which is a herb that was once taken by people as tea, but is now mostly reserved for cats. It would probably be impossible to find a cat that doesn't like its pinch of catnip. The herb makes old cats act young and young ones a little crazy. If you have ever seen the excited stretching and rolling of a cat with a new catnip mouse, you will know how true that is.

People have different scents, and cats know the smell of every person in the family. They like some people's smell better than others. If a person a cat likes puts a piece of clothing down, the cat will be lying on it in a minute.

It is through their noses that cats can tell at several feet

whether a visiting cat is a male or a female. And, of course, cats use their noses to get acquainted with new houses. Take them to a new home and you will see them sniff at everything. Then, when they leave and want to return, the familiar smells will help to guide them back.

Cats' eyes also are very keen, but it is not true that they can see in total darkness. It is also false that cats' eyes light up in the dark. They merely reflect any light that strikes them.

On the other hand, cats can see quite well in semidarkness, by moonlight or by the light of stars. This is because cats' eyes can make much better use of whatever light there is than our eyes can. In the cat's eyes the pupil, the opening through which light reaches the inner part of the eye, can expand much more than our pupil can. In an almost dark room, the pupil will open so wide as to fill almost the entire eye. You can see this by taking your cat into a room at night. Turn off the light, but allow just a little light to come in through the window. Once you are used to the darkness, look closely at your cat's eyes. They will seem almost completely black. The pupil has widened across the whole front of the eye. The same thing happens when a cat is anxious, scared, or sad.

In very bright light the cat's pupil contracts to a narrow vertical slit. This means that a cat is not nearly as dazzled by bright sunlight as we are. Even at high noon, when the sun shines at its strongest, a cat can see well enough not to miss a distant goal such as a wind-tossed leaf or a grasshopper.

Cats are excellent at judging distances by eye. A leaping cat seldom misses, whether it jumps from table top to table top or upon prey. Before jumping, it crouches, bottom up and tail twitching. Its eyes are gazing, fixed, measuring, until it is sure of making the perfect landing. It's really quite a trick, and all without a yardstick.

Can cats see colors the way we do? Even scientists are not sure. Some say cats see only black and white and gray; others believe that they see some colors. Many cat owners tell of cats who show a fondness for special colors. One cat always chose to lie on something red; another preferred to eat from a blue bowl. But perhaps it was the smell of these things that they preferred. All we can really be certain about is that if cats see color, they see it differently from us.

Its eyes are one of the most striking features of the cat. In ancient Egypt women outlined the shape of their eyes to resemble the cat's. And women still do this today. Cats' eyes may be green, blue, yellow, orange, or hazel. In healthy cats they are always very clear and shiny. Cats do not have eyelids. They can look directly into your eyes with their own eyes wide open and unblinking. When they want to close their eyes, they squeeze them shut.

The cat's sense of taste is not as keen as its other senses. Cats often cannot tell whether a food is poisoned, unless the smell tells them. But there is no doubt that cats like some foods more than others and that they enjoy different foods. Cats vary a lot in what they like to eat; some eat cookies and cereal and cheese and love them. Many are mainly meat and fish eaters and prefer a good piece of steak to anything.

The cat's tongue is a marvelous tool. Its entire surface is covered with tiny, hard spikes which make the tongue as rough as a piece of sandpaper. It is ideally suited for cleaning off sticky dirt or rasping the last shreds of meat off a bone. The cat's tongue is its washcloth and scrubbing brush, and the cat, being perhaps the cleanest animal in the world, makes much use of it.

Do you want to get the feel of your cat's tongue? That is easy. Most cats like butter and can be induced to lick some off your

finger. Many times too when a cat is busy licking itself, it will take your finger on too, if you just hold it there. But cats also often will lick your hand to show their love.

People used to think that the cat's tail helped it to balance. But this is not necessarily so. There are some tailless cats and they hold their balance as well as any with tails. Cats' tails can be short or long, thin or bushy, curled or straight. They mainly tell you a lot about how a cat feels.

The cat's beautiful body and its keen senses are masterminded by a brain that is very much like the human brain, only smaller. Because the structure of their brain is so similar, they do think quite a bit the way we do. Cats learn from experience, they can plan, and to some degree they can reason things out. Along with a well-developed brain, cats also have a delicate nervous system, which makes them some of the most alert and aware of the mammals. Without this sensitive nervous system, the feline personality would not be as engaging as it is.

The Cat's Personality

CATS THE WORLD OVER HAVE many things in common, just like people everywhere. Cats generally are curious, clean, playful, and smart. Most cats like to get up on fences and such things; they enjoy looking down on the world from high places; they love cozy fires and kind people. If they had their choice, most cats would love a warm, comfortable home during the day, to be followed by a night of adventure in fields and streets. But, like people, every cat leads a different kind of life, and every cat has its own personality.

Tennessee and Nanook, for example, are both tiger-striped cats with green eyes, but Nanook, who is Tennessee's daughter, is a much bigger cat. And in personality they are just as different as many human mothers and daughters. Tennessee, who was found in the mountains and was fierce and frightened at first, is now dainty, gentle, and sweet. She is very friendly to people and will approach any stranger who comes into the house where she lives.

Nanook was born in a city apartment and has had every comfort since birth; yet she is quite reserved toward people and easily upset by noise and quick movements. She is always hungry and impatient for her food.

At feeding time Tennessee sits very quietly, patiently watching every move her mistress makes with her large, green, almond-shaped eyes. Nanook meanwhile paces, paws, and claws and gives out loud hungry roars like a zoo lion at feeding time. And when the cats are taken to the country, Nanook, the city-bred cat, is the big hunter and explorer. Despite her size, she is as fast as lightning and can catch a grasshopper in mid-air. Tennessee, who is slender and country bred, hardly cares to catch a mouse. Even outdoors, she seldom leaves the sight of her owners.

Watch some of the cats you know, and you will soon discover that they can be as different from each other as people. It just takes an observant eye to see it. There are shy and bold cats, slow and fast ones. Some cats like to roam; others stay close to home. A few cats are water "bugs," even though most cats prefer to see water rather than feel it. One cat takes a swim every summer morning with its twelve-year-old master.

The Cat's Personality

All cats, however, are curious. You have no doubt heard that trite saying "Curiosity kills the cat." Actually it very seldom does. Curiosity is a very good trait and it seems odd that in stories and books curious creatures always get into trouble. More often curiosity leads to finding out all sorts of exciting things about the world in which we live.

Cats are curious about everything new. A cat in a new home will move about, slowly, from one piece of furniture to another, sniffing, pawing, feeling with its whiskers, until it is well acquainted with the whole house. Once the inside of the house is covered, the cat will want to explore the outside. It will not run off into the green. First it will stalk close to the house, smelling everything nearby to make sure the world here is safe and friendly and that it can find its way home again.

Any unfamiliar package in the house becomes an object of curiosity. The cat will edge up to it gingerly, often with arched back. When it is close enough, the cat will stretch out a front paw and touch the package ever so slightly, ready to run. If the package doesn't move, that's fine, and the cat is no longer so curious about it.

Cats are most curious about things that move. Some cats can sit for hours on a window sill and watch intently the movements of cars and people going by.

Creatures that are curious usually tend to be smart. Certainly cats are smart. Their intelligence shows in everything they do. Watch how a cat concentrates when it plays or hunts. It can block out all other noises and sights, fixing its whole mind and eye on that faraway mouse. Cats have a good memory too; they often remember people and favorite places for years. A lonely city tomcat was once befriended by a lonely old lady. She took him to her home, loved him and petted him, and then, to his horror, decided to shine up his fur with hair cream. The poor cat fled as fast as he could. Years later the same cat and lady met again. The cat recognized her at once. He went up to her, remembering her kindness, but as soon as she bent to pet him, he ran away. He had not forgotten what had happened the last time.

A cat's independence has a lot to do with how it learns, and independence is one quality that all cats share. But what is this independence, really? Do not mistake it for unfriendliness, as many people do. Happy cats are affectionate. They love the people who give them good homes and are kind to them. Such a cat hates to be without people. It will pursue its master or mistress from room to room and jump on their laps as soon as they sit down. But it will want to make its own decisions. It will not want to be picked up and held against its will.

And that is really what the cat's independence means. It is no coldness; it is a pride in being itself, a dislike of being bossed. Cats don't want to be forced into obedience; they hate the feel ing of being imprisoned. They may sit serenely on a lap fo hours and struggle and scratch as soon as you pick them up and enclose them in your arms.

But there too cats will be quite different. One cat may b much more sensitive about being held than another. Many o them allow small children to hold them and squeeze them bu wouldn't let an adult do it.

If you come across a cat that hisses or scratches as soon as yo come near it, you can be fairly sure that that cat has been badl treated or that it has had a homeless life. A cat that has lived i cold alleys, feeding on garbage, and sprinting from under cars often will be wild and unfriendly. Such a cat may run from people or lash out with a sharp front claw at the gentlest hand But if it is taken into someone's home and given kind treatment it usually turns into a tame and affectionate pet.

Like people, cats are not all equally sensitive. There are som crazy cats who just cannot get along with people, even whe they are treated very well.

Some people think that cats aren't as smart as dogs, becaus they cannot be taught tricks. Cats *do* learn tricks, and they ofter teach themselves many more. But they cannot be *forced* to lear tricks. They will learn when their mood is right for it, usually a part of a game.

Nanook's mistress once dropped a piece of paper accidentally and Nanook brought it back. She was praised and petted, and after that she retrieved a piece of paper that was thrown. Now retrieving paper balls is her favorite game. As soon as there is the sound of a piece of paper being crumpled, a thud on the floor announces that Nanook is aroused out of her sleep, off her perch, and ready to play. Tennessee has learned to jump on a bed to the snap of fingers. It just happened as her mistress played with her.

Most cats will sit up for a piece of meat, but that isn't much of a trick. One thing is certain: cats learn tricks only through love, petting, and rewards, never through spanking.

Cats will teach themselves a number of tricks. Almost every cat can open doors that aren't securely locked. They do this by wiggling knobs, pushing up latches, or clawing at the bottom of the door. Quite a few cats learn how to open nonmagnetic refrigerator doors between meals. Cats have many tricky ways of getting their owners to feed them, such as waking them up every morning by poking them gently on their noses with a paw. Some cats that prowl at night learn to scratch their owner's bedroom windows every morning. That's easy when the bedroom is on the ground floor. But cats have been known to climb up over the roof of a house and poke their heads upside down at the bedroom window.

Often, learning tricks is just part of a cat's playfulness. All cats are by nature playful. Kittens are always playful, and grown-up cats will be if you play with them. Sometimes a city cat that is never played with does forget how to be playful and prefers to sleep all day.

But many cats make up their own games even when nobody plays with them. Nanook often plays with drops of water plunging from a leaky faucet. She sits on the edge of the bathroom sink and tries to catch each drop with her paw. Tennessee, when she is ready to play, wanders about and sooner or later finds a small toy to bat around the floor.

Some cats' games are peculiar. One day in the winter a man watched a cat play in the snow. There seemed to be no bird or mouse to chase, nothing that the man could see the cat might be after. Nevertheless, the cat would crouch, then run up a tree trunk and right down again, over and over. The man thought that the cat might be practicing hunting. It probably just had to get rid of a lot of extra playfulness, or perhaps it saw something move that the man didn't see. But actually, hunting and playing are pretty much the same thing for a cat. A cat doesn't hunt because it is hungry. Even a well-fed cat will chase a mouse, simply because it's fun.

Most of the games that cats like to play are stalking, chasing, and pouncing games. A rattly piece of paper such as tin foil or wax paper, tied to a string and pulled gently along behind you, is almost as good as a live mouse. Cats also like ping-pong balls and catnip toys. But because catnip affects them so strongly, you should use it sparingly. Paper bags and cartons are also good

toys. Tennessee loves to be put under a grocery carton with holes in it, and to poke her paws at a stick or pencil that is pushed gently through the holes.

Cats often like teasing games like hide and seek. You could almost say they have a sense of humor. Some cats love to hide under a table and poke their owners with a paw as they walk by.

When two cats live in a house, they often play-fight with each other. It's a way of getting rid of stored-up energy, or tension from hunger, for it often happens close to mealtimes. Suddenly one hears a wild thumping and bumping, and finds two cats locked tightly in a mock battle, with fur flying and back paws scratching madly away at each other. It all looks very fierce and sounds more so, with growling, hissing, and mournful meowing. But when all is done, neither cat is hurt. This kind of friendly tumble is more likely to happen between apartment cats that don't get to go outside. Perhaps this helps them keep alive the wild, adventurous part of their nature.

At heart every cat is both tame and wild. Probably if a cat could have its own way, it would be a pet all day and a wild hunter all night. Quite a few cats in the country and in small towns live this way. Some people have special slats cut into a door, so the cat can come and go as it pleases. Others let the cat out at night and wake to its pawing and mewing early in the morning.

For most cats nighttime is the time for adventures and mating. It is at night that one often hears the noisy caterwauling of tomcats fighting for a pretty female. For when a female cat is in heat (that is, when she is ready to have kittens), she has a special smell that draws the tomcats from the whole neighborhood. If there is a fight, most likely the pretty female will mate with the winner. Sometimes she first hisses and spits a bit, but that is all an act; she really is happy to have found a mate. By morning male and female return to their own homes, gentle and tame, as though nothing had happened. They may never meet again, for tomcats are not very interested in kittens. The job of bearing them and training them is all left to the female cat.

The Cat's Personality

Few cats live the ideal outdoor-indoor life. Thousands of homeless cats roam city streets feeding off garbage. Most of them would probably gladly give up a good part of their freedom to have a warm home, good food, and tender hands to pet them. On the other hand, most family pets cannot be allowed to go out into city traffic.

Cats can be very contented living an indoor life, much more so than dogs. But if a cat is to be indoors all the time, it should be altered, so that it no longer feels the need to mate. A veterinarian, an animal doctor, performs this operation painlessly. In the case of a tomcat, one says he is neutered; in the case of a female cat, one says she is spayed.

In its wanderings a cat meets other animals, including other cats, and it is its relations with other animals that stir so much disagreement about our furry friend. Some people, for example, don't like cats because they prefer dogs, and they think cats always fight with dogs. But cats and dogs need not be enemies, and many of them happily share a home.

If you want to have a cat and dog, it is best to start out with a kitten and a puppy. Then they almost always become good friends. But if one of the pets is already grown up and is used to being the center of attraction, then the best you can hope for is that the two animals will learn to tolerate each other. Cats are jealous, and old-timers have to get used to the idea of a newcomer slowly. Sometimes cats are jealous of newborn babies If your family gets a new animal or baby, you should give your old cat as much petting and attention as it had before. Then it usually will accept the newcomer.

URSUS AMERICANUS

The Cat's Personality

There are many true-life stories of cat and dog friendships. One family tells of their cat, Fluffy, and a mongrel dog named Buddy. These two were inseparable. Where one went, the other followed. Then one day the dog became sick and had to be taken to an animal hospital. Fluffy missed her friend so much that she refused to eat until the dog came home.

Cats have made friends with all kinds of animals, even traditional prey like birds and mice. In one family the pet canary would fly out of his cage and light on the back of the cat. For a time, one of the bear cages in the Central Park Zoo, in New York was the favorite sunning spot of a whole family of cats. A cat may even protect prey if it belongs to its own master. One farm cat never chased the chickens on its farm, but quickly attacked any strange chicken that might wander onto its master's property.

Nobody likes to see a cat catch and kill a bird, but cats catch birds very seldom. In seven years of summer hunting, Nanook, fast as she is, has brought home only one bird. Some cat-lovers say that a cat can catch only a sick bird, that a healthy bird flies away too fast.

It is also good to remember that sometimes the cat is the prey of a bird. Not many cats are caught by birds, but woe to the cat that wanders alone near an eagle's nest. Cat meat is a favorite eagle meal. Owls too sometimes prey on cats.

People are quick to criticize animals, and forget that we ourselves kill and eat ducks, pheasants, and other wild game. Nature is set up that way. We live on plants and animals, and animals mostly must live on each other. It is sad to see a dead

bird or even a dead mouse, but the cat must follow its own nature; it is part of the whole arrangement of life, part of the great pattern we call "the balance of nature." Death makes room for new life; the number of all creatures has to be kept in check, or the world would become so clogged with them that nothing could move or live.

It really is amazing how often cats overcome their natural instinct to hunt prey. This is because they are so intelligent that they can change with the situation. A cat's strong mother instinct also may overpower any other feelings she might have. Cats are devoted and loving mothers, and nursing cats have adopted all kinds of strange baby animals. And not just because they have lost their own kittens. There is a famous photograph of a mother cat nursing three kittens and two baby rats.

Cats adjust easily to different kinds of life. They can be happy

The Cat's Personality

as pampered indoor pets or enjoy the adventures of the wild. They can survive in alleys, fields, and woods and readily become part of a family again. They can live with birds, dogs, and other "enemy" animals. They are jealous of their own living space and fend off other cats, but when many cats have to share a roof together, each has a great respect for the other's little private spot. Cats like to hunt alone, but when the need arises they may hunt in packs. Cats are often left behind in summer vacation spots by thoughtless owners. In the winter these cats are likely to roam together, cuddle up in sleep for warmth and share whatever food they find.

Cats know when people are kind to them, when a hurt is done on purpose or by accident. This is why so many cats are very patient with small children and sometimes allow themselves to be turned into toys.

Cats express their affection, their contentment, or their displeasure in so many different ways that one really needs to have an eye and an ear for a cat's language.

The Cat's Meow

ONE OF THE NICEST THINGS about a cat is its purr. There doesn't seem to be a sound that is more comforting and pleasing. The purr has turned many a former cat hater into a cat lover. What can be more cozy and restful than to sit in front of a fire with a purring cat at your feet?

Nobody is quite certain *how* the cat purrs. Some scientists think there are extra, false vocal chords in the cat's throat, and that these vibrate to make the purr. There is little doubt, however, as to *why* a cat purrs. A purring cat is a contented, well fed cat, and the best thing about the purr is that it makes you feel contented too.

The cat's purr is a steady, soft, churning noise. It sounds a lot like a car standing idle with the motor running. Some cats purr very loudly; others purr so softly that you can hardly hear them. You always can feel a cat's purr, though, by placing the palm of your hand against the cat's ribs or by holding a finger against its throat.

Some cats purr almost all day; others purr very little. Nanook breaks into a purr as soon as she is near her mistress or food. If she is near food it quickly turns into a loud, demanding "meow." Nanook's purr is very loud and shakes her whole body. She can be heard across a large living room. Tennessee's purr is quite soft. When Tennessee was first brought to a safe home after her sad mountain adventures, she did not purr. It was almost a year before she felt secure and happy enough to do so. Now she purrs often and easily.

Cats are expressive in many different ways. They can show all kinds of feelings in their faces, with their bodies, and with different tones of voice. Many cats, when they are well fed and contented, "pump" or "knead," with their front paws, along with purring. They first do this as kittens, when they are nursing at their mother. When they grow up, many cats knead their contentment into a pillow or any piece of soft clothing left about. Sometimes, if they are sitting on your lap, they will knead into your knee, and that isn't so pleasant. It feels a bit like being stuck with pins.

The cat's "meow" can mean many different things, and cats also make quite a few other noises with their throats. Some cats actually squeak, others chirp almost like birds. Tennessee squeaks, Nanook chirps. When she watches a bird from a windowsill, she opens her mouth and makes a strange little throaty chirp. It sounds as if she were trying to lure the bird near by imitating it but probably it is a sound of excitement.

People who live with cats soon find out what different meows mean. There is the deep-throated meow of hunger; it is quite different from the "Let-me-out" meow. The angry, shrieking meow of a cat who wants to scare away a prowling dog or strange cat is also very distinctive.

Some cats talk little and some cats chatter. Tennessee is a chatter cat. So are most Siamese cats. Tennessee actually has a kind of "I-love-you" meow. If she is lying down and her mistress merely comes close she usually looks at her with bright eyes and perked ears and makes a friendly "hello" meow. But if she really wants to sleep and doesn't want to be petted, her voice quite definitely says, "Leave me alone now."

Cats express their feelings with each other as well as with people. A mother cat uses many noises to teach her kittens about life. A kitten knows that the mother's growl means danger is near; it's time to hide near Mother. A cat with a mouse or a stolen piece of meat growls to keep away other cats—or a human being, if it thinks its morsel will be taken away. A cat's sounds can express fear and pain, and even loneliness. Tennessee used to wander with her owners in the woods of Maine. Sometimes she would lose sight of them, and then she would utter a low, sad wail, sounding very lonely. It always led them to her, and then the sound quickly changed into a happy, welcoming meow.

Cats' faces are very expressive. They can look open and trusting, sad or suspicious. The cat's eyes may be round or narrowed to tiny slits; its ears may point up with joy or lie flat against the back of the head. With its eyes narrowed and its ears flattened, a snarling cat can be a pretty fierce-looking creature. An angry cat also arches its back, and all the fur along the back of its spine

71

stands on end. The tail, high in the air and bushed out to three times its normal size, adds to the picture of strength and anger.

A cat's tail is also very expressive. Happy cats, especially those leaving a good dinner, or walking up to one, walk with tails high. But a tail can also wave back and forth slowly to show pleasure, and many a cat has lost a mouse by wagging its tail with excitement. A slightly annoyed cat may twitch its tail to let you know it would rather not be petted before it will finally get up and walk away.

Cats not only show affection by poking with their gentle paws but also punish kittens by slapping them with a paw. Licking is another way to show affection to people and other cats. A cat often rubs its whole body against one's leg to show fondness. Two cat friends living together will rub each other's whiskers, lick each other's ears, and curl up together to sleep.

Cats not only express many different feelings themselves but can understand a lot more of human tones and words than we generally think. They know by the sound of the human voice whether their masters are pleased or angry. Almost every cat will learn its name. Many cats also learn the name of every member of the family. Some cats have obeyed orders to wake up the children in a family. One cat got to know the name of a medicine it had to take regularly and would walk out of the room whenever it was mentioned. Nanook knows that the word "tweedle" means "Bat me back that piece of paper." It's hard to imagine how many actual words some cats will learn unless one lives with them.

Cats generally love to be talked to, especially in soothing voices. And there is no doubt that you and your cat can tell each other many things, if you listen and look and talk and touch.

Plain and Fancy Cats

CAT BREEDERS REFER TO PURE-bred cats as *fancy* cats and to ordinary alley cats as *plain* cats. You can buy several kinds of purebred cats, but plain cats still outnumber by far the fancy cats in our homes. And a plain cat can be as beautiful as any expensive purebred.

Fancy cats keep their special features only as long as they mate with their own kind. That is why there are cat breeders. If you have a female Siamese ready to have kittens, you can take her to a breeder who has the same kind of Siamese tomcat. But if a Siamese mates with a plain tomcat, she will give birth to plain kittens, looking very much more like the tomcat than like herself.

Cat breeders and *fanciers*, which is the word for people who show cats, are very particular about all the fine details of a cat's colors and markings, the shape and shade of its eyes, the form of its head, and other features. These are important mostly to people who want to buy expensive cats and show them.

A cat show is a good place to get a close look at the different breeds of cats. Cat shows are popular and frequent today. The first show was held in England almost 400 years ago. At that time cats were given prizes not so much for how they looked but for what they could do. One was given to the fastest mouser, that is, the cat who could catch a mouse first. But there also was a prize for the most beautiful cat.

Modern cat shows concentrate on beauty. Prizes are given to cats that are the finest specimens of particular groups.

Actually, the differences between cats are quite small. Compared with dogs, for example, they vary little in size and shape. Think of the great difference between a tiny, graceful chihuahua and the big, lumbering St. Bernard. There is no such variation between house cats.

Cats fall into three main groups: longhairs, domestic shorthairs, and foreign shorthairs. The original longhaired cats were called Angoras, because they came from Angora, the capital of Turkey. As a pure breed they are almost nonexistent today in the United States. Cats somewhat similar are called Persians or just longhairs. They come in pure black or white, tabby (striped), calico (having spots of color), tortoiseshell (with black, reddish, and cream blotches), and many other colors.

Longhaired cats are very luxurious. They make beautiful house pets but don't do so well on a farm. Can you imagine trying to untangle the burrs and bits of straw that a longhaired cat would catch on its prowls around the fields and barns? In any case, longhaired cats need a lot of careful grooming to keep their fur silky and smooth.

Plain and Fancy Cats

Their thick fur often makes longhaired cats look large and lazy. That's why many people think they aren't as bright as other cats and not as playful, but that is not true. A healthy longhaired cat is just as smart as any other kind of cat, and it can be very playful and an excellent hunter.

Under their heavy fur, longhaired cats have short, sturdy bodies and legs. Their heads are especially round and their eyes big. A Persian kitten is as fluffy as a dandelion puff.

The Maine cat is another longhaired cat. Its fur isn't nearly as plush as the true Persian's, but it has a bushy, striped tail like that of a raccoon, from which it gets the fun name "coon cat." Some breeders don't consider the Maine cat a breed, but one writer says that when Maine cats mate with each other they have Maine kittens, so they must be a breed. It is believed that the first Maine cats were crossbred from Angoras and shorthairs. In any case, the Maine cat is a native American.

PERSIAN

MANX

DOMESTIC SHORTHAIR

The domestic shorthair is really a plain cat that has been bred for pure color and the right shape of head and all the other fine points that cat-show judges look for. A black shorthair, for example, has to be pure black, just like a black Persian. Shorthairs come in the same variety of markings as the longhairs. This kind of cat is a real native American; in fact, a lot of our so-called alley cats would pass muster at a cat show as perfect specimens of domestic shorthairs. You might find a perfect tabby shorthair at your doorstep someday, but you also can buy one in a pet store.

ABYSSINIAN   SIAMESE

The most popular foreign shorthair is the Siamese. Once you have seen a Siamese you can recognize one anywhere. Its body color varies from off-white to a deep grayish brown, and its legs, tail, and face have a contrasting dark tone of blue-gray or brown. These are called seal point, silver point, or chocolate point, according to the shade of gray or brown. Large bright blue eyes shine out of the dark masks of their faces. Siamese cats are especially graceful and bright. People who own such cats find them loving and talkative. They make many different kinds of noises. Sometimes they cry as loudly as a hungry baby.

One very unusual cat seldom seen in this country but more often in England is the Manx, or tailless cat. The perfect Manx has only a dimple where its tail should be. A Manx cat that has a bump at its hind end instead of a tail is still accepted at a cat show, but it won't win any prizes for perfection. The true Manx comes from the Isle of Man in the Irish Sea. Manx cats have very long hind legs and they hop like rabbits when they run.

The cat of today that looks most like the Egyptian Kaffir cat is the Abyssinian. This cat is very rare in America. Abyssinian cats are very gentle and a little shy with strangers, but they are extremely affectionate with their owners. They are an even cinnamon brown, but each hair is ticked with three bands of color and the undercoat is orange. Their ears are rather large and their eyes have a beautiful almond shape.

Cats with a smooth, bluish-gray fur are generally known as blue cats. These are sometimes also called Maltese, British blues, or Russian blues. The most important thing about a blue is that it is bluish-gray all over, down to the soles of its paws.

A Burmese cat looks much like a Siamese except that it is chocolate brown all over and has yellow or turquoise eyes and a very glossy fur.

New breeds are sometimes developed by cat breeders. The Himalayan is one such new breed but it hasn't become very popular yet. A Himalayan is a combination of longhair and Siamese; it is, in fact, a longhaired Siamese.

Whether longhaired or shorthaired, plain or fancy, with eyes of blue, green, or orange, all cats take pretty much the same road in growing up.

From Kitten to Cat

KITTENS GROW INSIDE THE pregnant mother cat for about nine weeks. When the mother cat is ready to give birth she usually finds herself a quiet, dark, and private place. It might be an unusual place, too. Kittens have been born inside drawers, in haylofts, under stoves, and even in doghouses. One cat had her kittens inside a packing crate that was open when she got in and was afterwards nailed shut because no one knew that she was in it. She traveled all the way across the Atlantic from the United States to Europe, and to everyone's surprise arrived there safely with all the kittens alive.

Cat owners like to make up cozy boxes for their pregnant cats. This is all right as long as the box is big enough for the mother cat to stretch out in, and not so big that the kittens may not find the mother easily. But if someday you have a pregnant cat, don't be hurt if she ignores your cozy box and prefers a closet or a drawer. Remember, cats are independent. Tennessee had her first kitten in the middle of the kitchen floor. After that she was persuaded to get into a padded grocery box.

From Kitten to Cat

The kittens in a litter do not all arrive at once. Tennessee had her first three kittens within about five minutes of each other. Then there seemed to be no more, and her owners were very pleased. They had been promised homes for two kittens and were going to keep the third. They settled down with cups of coffee and let Tennessee get on with her job of cleaning the newborn kittens. Half an hour later they peeked into the box and there was number four, very new and wet. Thinking that was surely the end, they left the house. When they returned, Tennessee had given birth to kitten number five.

It is just as well that there is some time between the arrival of each kitten, because the mother cat has to do a good clean-up job on each one. Like all mammals, or nursing animals, each kitten is born inside a thin sack. The mother has to nip open the sack right away so that the kitten can breathe, and then dry and clean the wet, matted bundle of fur.

A tiny kitten is completely helpless, but fortunately cats are very devoted mothers. They love their work of cleaning and nursing their babies and seldom leave their newborn. Kittens spend all day huddled close to their mother's warm body, or nursing at her. Most cats have four pairs of nipples from which the whole litter can feed all at once, sucking and kneading happily.

Newborn kittens are born blind and should be kept in dark places. Bright light can hurt their eyes. Kittens usually open their eyes after two weeks, often earlier.

A kitten is an awkward, unbalanced little thing. Its legs are quite weak; its tail is short, and its head large and heavy com-

pared to the rest of the body. The kitten at first has a hard time holding up its head. But by about two months everything is pretty much in proportion, even though the kitten is still really a toddler, not very steady on its legs and not nearly as agile in climbing and cleaning itself as it will be when it is full grown. Once they can walk, kittens follow their mother about everywhere.

Most kittens start to purr for the first time after they are about a week old. They have to learn to feel secure and happy in this world.

84

Kittens, like grown-up cats, are probably the cleanest of all animals. At first the mother does all the licking in the hard-to-get-to places, but even at two weeks many kittens begin to wet their paws and wash their faces.

Kittens that are allowed to stay with their mother until they are six weeks old are usually toilet-trained by their mother. If they are outdoor cats, they go outdoors with the mother; if indoor, they follow mother to the bathroom and watch her use the toilet pan. A mother cat may carry her kittens to the bathroom by the scruff of the neck.

Like human babies, kittens are born without teeth. By the time they are three weeks old, a kitten's first teeth usually begin to show. This too is the time to start giving them solid food, like meat or fish. Cats, like people, start out with baby teeth that are later replaced by permanent teeth.

Everything that has been said about cats being curious and playful is true of kittens, only more so. A kitten is just about the most playful, mischievous, curious little creature in the world. It looks at everybody and everything with large, curious eyes and thinks of almost everything as a toy.

A kitten becomes a grown-up cat at about eight months. Very soon after that cats are ready to become parents themselves.

A cat's year is very different from a human year. It has been estimated that one cat year is about the same as seven human years, but that is not quite true. We know that a cat of one year is about like a child of three and that a seven-year-old cat is about as old as a 23-year-old person. So it is not surprising that cats die a lot sooner than we do. The average life span for a cat now is about fourteen years. But, like people, many cats are growing older, and 16 or 18 years is not an unusual age for a cat to reach. A few cats have lived as long as 25 and one or two have lived to 30.

Cats don't show age until they become very old. Then they grow gray and shrink a bit. Most old cats sleep all day and become less playful.

Nobody is quite sure what makes cats have a very long life, but love and good food have a lot to do with it; there's no doubt about that.

You and Your Pet

THERE ARE MANY WAYS TO GET a cat. Sometimes the cat gets you. You may meet one in the street; you may find one under your Christmas tree, or one may settle on your doorstep some morning and not go away. It's happened many times. But getting a pet is usually a family affair. It is generally best to start with a kitten. Older cats tend to be set in their ways and sometimes they pine away for their first owners. Of course, if you just happen to fall in love with a straggly old tomcat that you find munching in an overturned garbage can, that's all right. He could turn out to be a perfectly lovely pet.

Kittens can be bought and they can be had free. A friend may have an extra kitten; there are newspaper ads for free kittens, and the local animal shelters usually have quite a selection. Fancy cats generally have to be bought—in pet stores, at catteries (breeding homes), or at cat shows.

The kitten you bring home should be weaned—that is, it should be at least six weeks old and thus no longer need its mother's milk; and it should have all its teeth. Pick a kitten that

looks bright, perky, and curious; avoid one that seems very shy or hisses when you come near it. A healthy kitten seems as light as a feather and struggles and kicks when you try to hold it. Choose the kitten that you like the most, and if it matters to you, be sure to ask whether it is a male or a female cat.

A kitten is so cute and cuddly that you may want to hold it and fondle it all the time, but it is much better not to. Kittens in particular need a lot of sleep, so never disturb a sleeping kitten; also, for a kitten, playing with balls and toys is better than a lot of handling. Always be sure to put it down gently as soon as it wants to be let free. This way neither you nor the kitten will be hurt. Whenever you pick up a cat of any age, take it under the chest and front legs; and be sure to support its hind legs, for cats hate to be left with their hind legs dangling. Never pick up a cat by the scruff of its neck, not even a kitten. The mother cat can do this because she knows exactly how to hold the delicate kitten without breaking its neck. People can seldom be as gentle about this as the mother cat. Kittens are fragile and should be lowered gently to the floor, not dropped from arm height.

A piece of string with paper, a ping-pong ball, perhaps a catnip mouse, are good toys for a kitten. Cats love to play with a string-paper toy hung from a doorpost so that it barely clears the ground. They will leap and lunge at this for hours.

You also may want to fix up a special sleeping box or basket for your new pet, but don't be surprised if it ignores your efforts, especially if you place it in it; cats like to do their own discovering. If you put an old and unwashed piece of your clothing in the box it will probably feel more attracted to it.

A cat quickly learns its name. You will be surprised how soon yours will answer your call. Just call it by its name whenever you feed it. Kittens need about four meals a day. A grown-up cat will do fine on no more than two.

Cats need quite a variety of food. They eat meat, fish, eggs, cheese, and some vegetables. It's a good idea to get them used to all these foods right at the start. Like people, cats want different meals from day to day. You can feed them canned cat food at one meal and raw hamburger or beef kidney at another meal. Some table scraps with meat and green beans are fine too. Kittens should have milk at least once a day, but not all grown-up cats drink milk. It is very important always to have a little bowl of clean water about, so your cat can drink at any time.

If your kitten is six weeks old when you get it, it is probably house-trained. If not, it will soon learn. If there is a yard, let it out as often as you can at first. Most likely the kitten will let you know right away when it wants to go out. If the kitten is to be trained for indoors, it should have a pan in a special place, usually in the bathroom. The pan should have shredded paper, sawdust, or special sand that can be bought in most grocery stores. For a day or so you may need to carry your kitten regularly to the box, but it will very soon sniff it out for itself.

Cats do not need baths, unless they fall into something unusually dirty. They keep themselves clean. But it is a good idea to brush your cat every day. Most cats like to be brushed, so that is fun for the cat and for you.

When you get your kitten, you should ask whether it has been inoculated against enteritis, a virus disease that kittens can easily catch. If it hasn't, be sure your family takes the kitten to a veterinarian. Enteritis is the one disease that kills many cats, and a couple of shots will protect your kitten against it.

If you take good care of your cat you will seldom have to take it to a doctor. Cats are generally very healthy. They may be bothered by certain microbes or worms now and then, but they don't catch our colds, and we seldom catch anything from them.

Traveling or moving with a cat isn't very difficult. Cats are not enthusiastic about traveling, but some really get to like it. Most cats prefer to go places inside a nice, cozy, dark box or a special cat carrier. If you go to a summer vacation place, let your cat out to become acquainted with the new house soon after arriving. It's a good idea to keep it inside the new house for a couple of days, however, so that it knows the smells and sounds of the household and will not get lost when it goes outside.

Cats are delightful pets to have anywhere, but they are ideal for city apartments. They are quiet, clean, and contented. They do not have to be walked like dogs, and if left alone for a day or so they are happy enough if someone feeds them. Cats ask really very little of us. They are grateful for a warm home, regular food, and a master who allows them to be themselves.

Perhaps this is the most important thing about having any pet, to learn to understand its nature and accept it for what it is. Animals are not people, and they are not toys; they are delightful, unique creatures in their own right. If we see them this way, they can add much pleasure to our lives.